The Red Balloon

Eduardo Amos
Ernesto Pasqualin
Elisabeth Prescher

2nd edition

CB003196

Richmond

Richmond

Diretoria: *Paul Berry*
Gerência editorial: *Sandra Possas*
Coordenação de arte: *Christiane Borin*
Coordenação de revisão: *Estevam Vieira Lédo Jr.*
Coordenação de produção gráfica: *André Monteiro, Maria de Lourdes Rodrigues*
Coordenação de *bureau*: *Américo Jesus*
Coordenação de produção industrial: *Wilson Troque*

Consultoria de língua inglesa: *Marylou Bielenstein*
Assistência editorial: *Gabriela Peixoto Vilanova*
Revisão: *Denise Ceron*
Projeto gráfico de miolo e capa: *Ricardo Van Steen Comunicações e Propaganda Ltda./Oliver Fuchs*
Ilustrações de miolo e capa: *Roko*
Edição de arte: *Claudiner Corrêa Filho*
Tratamento de imagens: *Fábio N. Precendo*
Diagramação: *Tânia Balsini*
Pré-impressão: *Helio P. de Souza Filho, Marcio H. Kamoto*
Impressão e acabamento: *Coan Indústria Gráfica Ltda.*
Lote: *278433*

Dados Internacionais de Catalogação na Publicação (CIP)
(Câmara Brasileira do Livro, SP, Brasil)

> Amos, Eduardo
>   The red balloon / Eduardo Amos, Ernesto
> Pasqualin, Elisabeth Prescher. —
> 2. ed. — São Paulo : Moderna, 2005. —
> (Modern readers ; stage 1)
>
>
>   1. Inglês (Ensino fundamental) I. Pasqualin,
> Ernesto. II. Prescher, Elisabeth. III. Título. IV. Série.

04-8839   CDD-372.652

Índices para catálogo sistemático:
1. Inglês : Ensino fundamental   372.652

ISBN 85-16-04484-X

RICHMOND
EDITORA MODERNA LTDA.
Rua Padre Adelino, 758 — Belenzinho
São Paulo — SP — Brasil — CEP 03303-904
Central de atendimento ao usuário: 0800 771 8181
www.richmond.com.br
2019

Impresso no Brasil

Chapter 1

Andy Wayne is very happy today. It is the first day of his summer vacation.

He is happy for another reason, too. He is going on a trip to his grandfather's farm. The trip is a present from his parents because he is a good student.

Andy and his mother are in his bedroom now.

Mrs. Wayne — Is everything ready, Andy?

Andy — Yes, Mom. My clothes, boots, bag. Everything is okay.

Mrs. Wayne — I'm a little nervous.

Andy — Why, Mom?

Mrs. Wayne — This is your first trip alone.

Andy — Oh, come on. I'm so happy! Airplanes are very safe.

Mrs. Wayne — Sure, dear. You're right.

Mr. Wayne — Andy! Alice! Where are you? We're late! Hurry up!

Andy — We're up here, Dad. I'm ready. Let's go!

Glenn Wayne is Andy's grandfather. He is an old adventurer and explorer. His house is on a farm, far from the city. There is a lake in front of the house and many trees around it.

There are deer, rabbits, and birds near Grandpa Wayne's lake every morning. They aren't afraid of him. He's their friend.

Everything is ready for Andy's visit: the boat is at the dock; Yellow Star, the new horse, is in the stable; there is a nice chocolate cake on the kitchen table. Glenn Wayne is eager to see his grandson.

Suddenly, there is a noise outside. Andy is at the door now.

Andy — Bye, Mr. Brian, and thanks for the lift.

Mr. Brian — You're welcome. Bye, Andy. Bye, Glenn!

Andy — Hi, Grandpa!

Grandpa Wayne — Hello, Andy. I'm glad you're here. Oh, my! You're so tall! How are you? Are you hungry? Are you tired from the trip? How's your mother? And your father? What about school?

Andy — Hey, just a minute, Grandpa. Too many questions! First, ... here's a present for you.

Grandpa Wayne — Thank you, Andy. Oh, boy! What a nice hat!

Chapter 2

In the evening, after dinner, Andy and his grandfather are in the living room.

Andy — What's that in this picture, Grandpa?

Grandpa Wayne — That's my first balloon, the Blue Cloud.

Andy — And who's that man?

Grandpa Wayne — My father, and that's me near the balloon.

Andy — What about this balloon on the table?

Grandpa Wayne — It's a model of my new balloon, the Sky Lady.

Andy — It's neat, Grandpa. Is it here at your house?

Grandpa Wayne — Well, that's a surprise for tomorrow. It's bedtime now.

Grandpa Wayne (from out of the house) — Wake up, Andy Wayne! It's seven o'clock!

Andy (at the window) — What's that, Grandpa?

Grandpa Wayne — It's the Sky Lady. She's ready. Hurry up! Let's go.

Andy — Where?

Grandpa Wayne — Let's go up! Up in the sky!

Andy — Wow! Great, Grandpa! Let's go!

Soon, the balloon is up in the sky. The view is fantastic: a beautiful sight with rivers, animals and the marshland. There is a warm soft summer breeze. Andy is surprised, excited, and fascinated. What a fantastic morning!

8

Grandpa Wayne — Look, Andy. Look at those egrets on that tree.

Andy — Is that the Black River?

Grandpa Wayne — Yes, and the other one is the Miranda River. Look at the color of the waters.

Andy — They're different colors. The Black River is dark blue and the Miranda River is brown. Wow! Look at those macaws.

Grandpa Wayne — Those are blue macaws. They're an endangered species. There are other endangered species in this area, like those deer near the lagoon.

Andy — What a shame! They are so delicate.

Chapter 3

Hours later, the balloon is still in the sky. But the view is completely different. Andy and his grandfather are shocked.

Andy — Oh, no! That's horrible! Dozens of dead crocodiles on the riverbank. But why?

Grandpa Wayne — Crocodile skins are very valuable. There are many illegal hunters in this area.

Andy — Isn't that a hunters' camp?

Grandpa Wayne — Yes.

Andy — They look unfriendly, Grandpa.

Grandpa Wayne — Unfriendly? They are really dangerous!

Suddenly the balloon begins to fall.

Andy — What's the problem with the balloon, Grandpa?

Grandpa Wayne — There are holes. Bullet holes. We're in trouble, Andy. Big trouble.

The balloon is on the ground now.

Grandpa Wayne — Are you okay, Andy?

Andy — No, my leg is hurt.

Grandpa Wayne — Wait here. My neighbor Brian's farm is near here. He is a good friend. There's a radio on his farm.

Andy — But, Grandpa, it's dark. It's dangerous.

Grandpa Wayne — Quiet now, Andy. The hunters are close.

Andy — Okay, Grandpa. Go now!

Chapter 4

It is very dark now. This is a terrible night for Andy. He is tired, cold, and hungry. He is scared, too.

All the hunters from the camp are after Andy and his grandfather. Some are in boats. Many are on foot.

1st hunter — Here's the balloon.

Leader — What about the man and the boy?

1st hunter — There's nobody here, just the balloon.

2st hunter — Maybe they're somewhere in the river. Maybe they're dead.

1st hunter — Yes, probably.

Leader — Well, let's go back to the village.

2st hunter — No, not to the village. The police are probably there.

1st hunter — What about Monkey Island?

Leader — Good idea! Let's go to Monkey Island, men!

It's very early morning now. There's a loud noise in the sky. Grandpa Wayne is with the police in a helicopter.

Grandpa Wayne — Are you okay, Andy? Where are the hunters?

Andy — They're on Monkey Island.

Half an hour later, the helicopter and two police boats are also on Monkey Island.

Sergeant Brown — Are all the hunters here?

Soldier — Yes, sergeant. And their leader, too.

Grandpa Wayne — Good job, officer. The whole gang is out of action.

Sergeant Brown — This gang is out of action, but there are many other hunters around. The poor animals are still in danger.

KEY WORDS

The meaning of each word corresponds to its use in the context of the story (see page number, 00)

adventurer (4) aventureiro
afraid (4) temeroso
alone (3) sozinho
bedtime (6) hora de dormir
begin (10) começar
boat (5) barco
boot (3) bota
breeze (8) brisa
bullet (10) bala
cake (5) bolo
close (11) perto
cloud (6) nuvem
danger (9) perigo
dark (9) escuro
dead (10) morto
deer (4) veado
dock (5) cais
dozen (10) dúzia
eager (5) ansioso
early (13) cedo
egret (9) garça
endangered (9) ameaçado
every (3) todo
everything (3) tudo
excited (8) interessado
explorer (4) explorador
farm (3) fazenda
foot (12) pé
grandpa (4) avô
grandson (5) neto
ground (11) chão
half an hour (13) meia hora
hat (5) chapéu
hole (10) buraco
hungry (5) faminto
hunter (10) caçador
hurt (11) machucado
island (12) ilha
just (5) apenas
lake (4) lago
late (3) atrasado

leader (12) líder
lift (5) carona
loud (13) alto
macaw (9) arara
marshland (8) pântano
model (6) modelo; miniatura
neat (6) legal
neighbor (11) vizinho
nobody (12) ninguém
noise (5) barulho
out (7) fora
outside (5) fora
parents (3) pais
ready (3) pronto
riverbank (10) margem do rio
safe (3) seguro
scared (12) assustado
sight (8) vista
skin (10) pele
sky (6) céu
soft (8) suave
somewhere (12) em algum lugar
soon (8) logo
still (10) ainda
suddenly (9) de repente
sure (3) certo
those (9) aqueles
trouble (10) problema
unfriendly (11) hostil
vacation (3) férias
valuable (10) valioso
wait (11) esperar
wake up (7) acordar
whole (13) inteiro

Expressions
Hurry up! (3) Apresse-se!
Oh, come on! (3) Ora, vamos!
Oh, my! (5) Puxa vida!
What a shame! (9) Que pena!
You're welcome. (5) De nada.

ACTIVITIES

Chapter 1

A. Choose the correct answer.

1. Andy's present is
   a) his first day of vacation.
   b) a trip to his grandfather's farm.
   c) a bag with clothes and boots.

2. Mrs. Wayne is a little nervous because
   a) it is Andy's first trip alone.
   b) airplanes are very safe.
   c) Andy is late.

3. Grandpa Wayne is
   a) an adventurer.   b) a hunter.   c) a police officer.

B. Answer these questions about Chapter 1.

1. Where is Grandpa Wayne's house?
2. Why aren't the animals afraid of Grandpa Wayne?
3. Is everything ready for Andy's visit?

Chapter 2

A. Choose the correct answer.

1. After dinner, Andy and his Grandpa are
   a) in the stable.   b) at the door.   c) in the living room.

2. The Sky Lady is
   a) Andy's grandmother.
   b) Grandpa Wayne's first balloon.
   c) Grandpa Wayne's new balloon.

3. At seven in the morning, Andy is
   a) near the lake.   b) at the window.   c) in the living room.

B. Answer these questions about Chapter 2.

1. Who are the people in the picture on Grandpa Wayne's wall?
2. What color are the waters of the Black River and the Miranda River?
3. What are two endangered species near Grandpa Wayne's farm?

Chapter 3

A. Choose the correct answer.

1. Now, the view from the balloon is
   a) shocking.   b) beautiful.   c) fantastic.

2. The hunters are
   a) valuable.   b) friendly.   c) dangerous.

3. The balloon is on the ground. Andy is
   a) happy.   b) hurt.   c) okay.

B. Answer these questions about Chapter 3.

1. Why are Andy and Grandpa Wayne shocked?
2. Why are crocodiles endangered?
3. Why are Andy and Grandpa Wayne in trouble?

Chapter 4

A. Choose the correct answer.

1. The night is
   a) fantastic for Andy.
   b) terrible for Andy.
   c) calm for Andy.

2. It is night. The hunters are after
   a) the crocodiles.
   b) their leader.
   c) Andy and his grandfather.

3. Who is in the balloon?
   a) Nobody is.
   b) Andy is.
   c) Andy and Grandpa Wayne are.

B. Answer these questions about Chapter 4.

1. How is Andy in the night?
2. Where are the hunters at the end of the story?
3. That gang is out of action. Why are the animals still in danger?